Sleeps With Knives

Sleeps With Knives

Has It Hit You Yet? + a special essay: Earth Tribes at the Millennium

Trace L Hentz

BLUE HAND BOOKS | BLUE INDIANS COLLECTIVE
GREENFIELD MASSACHUSETTS

Native American Prose and Poetry

Hentz, Trace L [1956-]

ISBN: 978-0-578-58522-2

Family Photos are the property of the author.

Publisher: BLUE HAND BOOKS, Blue Indians Collective, 25 Keegan Lane, Greenfield, MA 01301, www.bluehandbooks.org

Published in the United States

Contents

words and lyrics

Trace L Hentz

from Becoming (an earlier work)

"

what matters most
is how well you
walk through the
fire

-Charles Bukowski

Preface

of my deep secret lands of poetry… and of course prose… and a few short memoir pieces from my chapbook "Becoming."

One of my rules for writing: Don't repeat yourself. Excuse me in this volume—because **some** of my words are yelled and repeated for effect.

This may sound RATHER funny but I do not consider myself a poet but I string together GOOD WORDS, like hip hop poetry, my own alchemy.

This book is for my granddaughters Cami and Aubrey, close family, old friends, new friends. It was time for me to collect words called poems (again) and do

College age me

this new chapbook seven years later. This is the second edition of SLEEPS WITH KNIVES | *Has It Hit You Yet?* The first edition was under my pen-name Laramie Harlow.

There is a long essay in this book ***Earth Tribes*** at the Millennium, which I wrote after a dream many years ago.

I collect names: given names, my adoptee name, created

names, married names, nicknames, catholic names, the name I pray with, the official driver's license name and the passport name. The name Lara I chose for me. My missing mother named me Laura Jean Thrall on my original birth certificate.

I never met my mother Helen, though I did meet my grandmother Helen (in secret in 1993).

Eventually I gave myself a gift, a name, a power I will use whenever I need it.

After 10 years of marriage, I took my husband's last name legally. He was happy.

In this way the pen (and my keyboard) is my weapon, a form of exorcism or retribution for what really happened.

On many occasions I call my poet self "Sleeps with Knives" because I have met sharks and monsters.

Maybe you met some, too.

There is big danger out there. We must all learn to navigate better.

lala

Sleeps with Knives

poems by Laramie Harlow

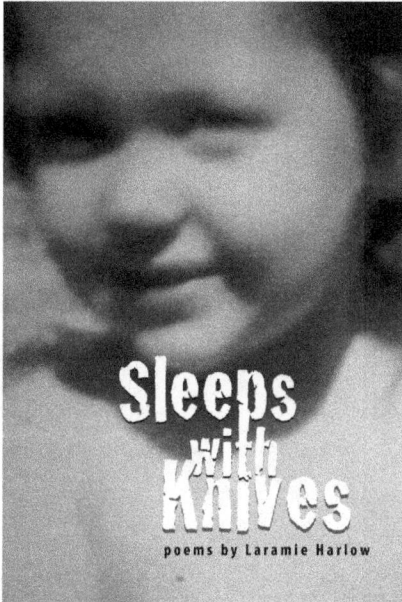

…this cover was my first chapbook back in 2012.

…Rae calls me lala

…the words/poems are dreams, crispy wisps of truth.

Ever think of humans as part of an experiment? I do.

Has it hit you yet? The internet is a very dangerous highway and people get robbed and people steal shit. It's broken bad, please fix it.

We're like elephants on a short chain. Mentally we don't think we can move.

In this regard, we think small.

I don't like it that I'm starting to shorten everything I write.

"A word after a word after a word is power…" —Margaret Atwood

02019

I had a dream I was outside on a hillside, and there were many cars with
many people, people chatting, walking their dog, going to work.
But I see a wave of energy... something they didn't see.
It hits them.
Eventually it also hits them that something happened - it doesn't kill.
It transforms.

ESKIMO (ANONYMOUS)

An Eskimo poet, who will forever remain anonymous, composed a song based on a legend of origins from the oral tradition.

MAGIC WORDS

In the very earliest time,
when both people and animals lived on earth,
a person could become an animal if he wanted to
and an animal could become a human being.
Sometimes they were people
and sometimes animals
and there was no difference.
All spoke the same language.
That was the time when words were like magic.
The human mind had mysterious powers.
A word spoken by chance
might have strange consequences.
It would suddenly come alive
and what people wanted to happen could
       happen—
all you had to do was say it.
Nobody could explain this:
That's the way it was.

Translated from the Inuit by Edward Field

other books by author

Mental Midgets | Musqonocihte
　One Small Sacrifice The Memoir
　Two Worlds: Lost Children of the Indian Adoption Projects
　Called Home: The RoadMap
　Stolen Generations
　Sleeps with Knives (2012)
　Becoming (retired 2019) (using penname Laramie Harlow)
　Unraveling the Spreading Cloth of Time: Indigenous Thoughts
concerning the Universe (with MariJo Moore)

1492

As children we were taught to memorize this year with pride and joy as the year people began living full and imaginative lives on the continent of North America.

Actually, people had been living full and imaginative lives on the continent of North America for hundreds of years before that. 1492 was simply the year sea pirates began to rob, cheat, and kill them.

—**Kurt Vonnegut,**
Breakfast of Champions

BEWARE OF
IMAGES

words and lyrics

rocket bodies

Circling
   Whirling
   Litter
   What was that?
   A meteor? No.
   Space Junk (aka orbital debris)
   Man-made space garbage
   Probably some old rocket bodies and dead satellites
   thousands of pieces in pounds and tons of danger
   Smaller bits: paint chips that flake away from the outsides of
devices, nuts and bolts, garbage bags, a lens cap, screwdriver, and
even a spatula.*
   Falling faster than a speeding bullet
   Waiting to hit
   Anywhere
   Anytime
   While you're driving
   When you're sleeping

   HOW WHAT WHEN WHERE HOW WHY
   How did this happen?
   What solution? Is there a solution?
   When will we hear about this on the news?
   Where is the warning light?
   How about a magnetic space junk garbage truck?
   WHY NOT?

   *2019: National Geographic: Experts predict an increasing
threat of space junk that will fall to Earth.
   A Forgotten Piece of Space Junk is Headed for Earth: The

object could be a lost piece of a rocket dating back to the Apollo missions

A new radar system will **track** 250,000 tiny pieces of **space junk**.

YOU had One Chance

Let me ask you
   Did your granddad fight in the Civil War?
   Or your great-great granddad?
   Do you even know?
   Of course not.
   How many slaves did he own?
   Where do your people come from – North, South, East, West?
   Were your ancestors immigrants and from where?
   And you should know who they fought and what they fought for
but
   Your parents were too busy raising you apparently and too tired
while trying to make money.

   You had one chance
   During the school years
   To get shit straight
   Wait, what did you get in your history class?
   Watered-down slavery
   No mention of the 1000 Indian Wars
   Or maybe dead (invisible) Indians
   How America is the greatest?
   The greatest what?
   What a crock of the perfect mess.

   We can all thank Big Publishing Houses
   Who still print big expensive history books that no one reads
   Except other Professors
   Who know their system is working
   to perpetuate crimes against humanity and injustice and racism
   Always failing People-of-Color on paper and in person
   Denying what really happened (and is still happening)

The theft
Genocide
Murder
Is still hidden history
That we cannot afford to read

"Human history becomes more and more a race between education and catastrophe."

has it hit you yet?

I am a dangerous woman.
  I **am** dangerous.
  I sleep with weapons.
  My life is full of danger.
  I sleep with a machete.
  I sleep with knives.
  I will kill you.
  I don't care if you like me.
  I am a dangerous woman.
  Has it hit you yet?
  I am a dangerous woman.

the cosmos and the snakes

Remember:
    There is a higher war:
    a cosmic war between higher intelligences
    between rulers and leaders
    dragging on, lasting centuries
    between the good ones and the evil ones.

    Remember:
    You and I have tangled with snakes
    and were bit many times, too many times
    Their kind of toxin
    can't kill but pollute our minds
    These monsters do twist reality into
    dreams, hallucinations, sweat:
    fear-raising hell, they create,
    negative emotions are like fuel

    Remember:
    Their playbook is chaos, fear:
    they will threaten each other to confuse us,
    all to scare "us" to death, give up
    and even drop a bomb to threaten our lives,
    our peace
    and I do see myself
    dancing with those devils

    Remember:
    We The People are not stupid.
    Their playbook has been: count on lazy poisoned
    brains to give power over to them,
    our brains corrupted.

We spend too much time on stupid.
Technology is a weapon.
Their playbook is not working now.

Remember:
good **will** prevail over evil and
whoever is patient for the end of war,
and will fight against it
will survive
We might be poor sad creatures
never quite understanding
what got us into this mess

Remember:
Life is more habit than creation
Swirling in mass
curling around each other
it's like evolution rewinds and goes
backwards, all the way back…

Remember:
Our cosmos has many menus
for all sorts of appetites
the rich ones think they'll eat us for lunch
but they're too dense, too blind, too blonde
not awake

Remember:
The earth is a park and **God** is our ranger

I may look starved, empty, lost
But they are all wrong
Only the wise are ever full
and drink air like perfume

God has many names. You should learn them all.
[It's a manifestation of the ongoing civil war among the elites]

Protocols of the Wise Men of Zion

Protocol 10: "It is from us that all-engulfing terror proceeds. We have in our service persons of all opinions: monarchists, demagogues, socialists trying to overthrow all established authority. By these acts all states are in torture; they exhort tranquility, are ready to sacrifice anything for peace. But we don't give them peace until they openly acknowledge our international super-government, and with submissiveness to utterly exhaust humanity with dissension, hatred, struggle, envy and even by use of torture, by starvation, by inoculation of diseases, by want, so that the goyim see no other issue than to take refuge in our complete sovereignty in money."

The Protocols were a manifesto written by a secret society that claimed itself superior to the rest of mankind, using the Hebrew word *goyim* (cattle) to refer to the masses (human beings).

awake

First thing:
   awake
   each morning
   I put out tobacco
   then face four directions of our mother
   I envision the polar bears, porpoises, timber wolves, buffalo,
   hummingbirds, birds, bumblebees, bats
   and all the others who are hurting
   because of humans
   and their need to destroy everything for profit.
   I pray for all living things. . .
   Mitakuye oyasin, my relatives
   It's me winyan ohmanisa waste la ke
   Good morning…

my church

(for Joan who left us)
  My church is made of snow
  My church is made of pine trees and lilac bushes
  My church is filled with singing birds and little creeks
  My church is a flock of geese and a soaring hawk
  My church is right outside my door
  I sing for all that is...
  I do not need a building to pray for all my relations
  I do not need anyone to tell me how to remember
  I do not need a book of words for my gratitude or loss
  I do not need a monsignor to bless me or forgive me
  I do not need to be reminded of Great Mystery who many call
GOD
  My church is open, vast and wide,
  just as my heart is open, vast and wide
  I will remember my friend Joan whose spirit has left us,
  who once looked for a building to pray and people to pray
with...(and was kicked out)
  then she found her church in her paintings of ducks and
wildflowers
  I only have to look at her canvas
  I only have to look at the snow, trees, birds and oceans
  to remember her
  I only have to see a sunflower
  to remember all that is her essence...

Kent, Washington (c) 2009 (November 5)

being (108 delusions)

Our ancestors left their trace
   in our blood, bones and DNA.
   Essence is our true identity;
   for being is born
   in the octaves of creation.
   You develop knowledge.
   Your Being attracts
   experiences you need.
   When you awaken
   through a succession of events,
   you have the capacity of genuine doing.
   With new knowledge of Being,
   change is possible.
   What a world we have imagined,
   What illusions we create.

So remain humble.
© 2004

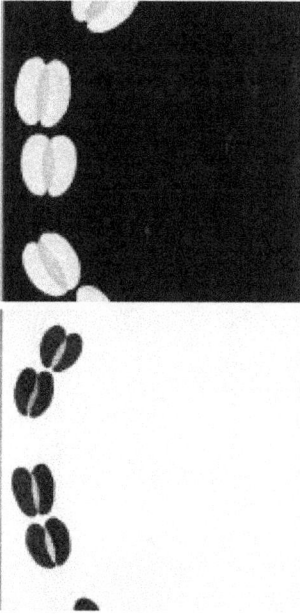

Buddhism tradition talks about the 108 earthly desires in mortals, 108 lies humans tell and 108 human delusions: in Tibet it is believed that there are 108 sins or 108 delusions of the mind:

abuse, aggression, ambition, anger, arrogance, baseness, blasphemy, calculation, callousness, capriciousness (unaccountable changes of mood or behavior), censoriousness (being severely critical of others), conceitedness, contempt, cruelty, cursing, debasement, deceit, deception, delusion, derision, desire for fame, dipsomania (alcoholism characterized by intermittent bouts of craving), discord, disrespect, disrespectfulness, dissatisfaction, dogmatism, dominance, eagerness for power, effrontery (insolent or impertinent behavior), egoism, enviousness, envy, excessiveness, faithlessness, falseness, furtiveness, gambling, garrulity (tediously talking about trivial matters), gluttony, greed, greed for money grudge, hardheartedness, hatred, haughtiness, high-handedness, hostility, humiliation, hurt, hypocrisy, ignorance, imperiousness (assuming power or authority without justification), imposture (pretending to be someone else in order to deceive), impudence, inattentiveness, indifference, ingratitude, insatiability, insidiousness, intolerance, intransigence (unwilling or refusing to change one's views or to agree about something), irresponsibility, jealousy, know-it-all, lack of comprehension, lecherousness, lying, malignancy, manipulation, masochism, mercilessness, negativity, obsession, obstinacy, obstinacy, oppression, ostentatious, pessimism, prejudice, presumption, pretense, pride, prodigality (spending money or using resources freely and recklessly), quarrelsomeness, rage, rapacity (being aggressively greedy or grasping), ridicule, sadism, sarcasm, seduction, self-denial, self-hatred, sexual lust, shamelessness, stinginess, stubbornness, torment, tyranny, unkindness, unruliness, unyielding, vanity, vindictiveness, violence, violent temper, voluptuousness, wrath.

We have much karmic debt to overcome... TLH

Buffalo Tracks artwork: Gay Meyers

as you have all along

Some lost their children
   some cried, anguished, mourned
   There was nothing you could do
   to stop them
   or stop their judgments
   trauma focuses the mind on survival

   Fill our hearts
   as you have all along
   Send us messages to be strong
   as you have all along
   Help us to be good people, good messengers
   as you have all along

   Grandmothers,
   generous with love and guidance, stay with us
   I felt peace, an inner smile, safe
   You helped me endure when I could not see you
   yet I heard you
   when I was sad, empty, weak, in pain
   You stayed, and I heard your quiet voices.
   Stay with me now
   As you have all along. . .
   I knew nothing about adoption when I started doing research.
   Are we like the mouse or monkey or frog or lion who will adapt
to a life of captivity and cages?

the last few hundred or so

humans were hijacked
   blindfolded
   handcuffed
   forced to kneel
   handed books
   given tests
   told lies
   cajoled
   demeaned
   ridiculed
   hair cut off
   tongues washed
   humiliated
   clothes burned
   brain washed
   torn apart
   tortured
   murdered
   . . . . in the name of GOD
   in the last few hundred centuries or so

sideroads

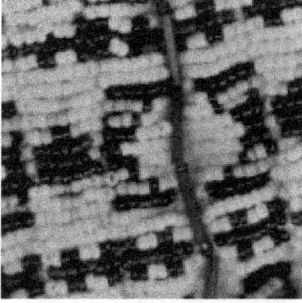

The decision to go
eyes wide open
I heard many myths are stupid
There might be no warm reception
Blood relationships are important, vital
yet to me utter strangers
in reunion
Because there are too many (white) Indians now
I'd have to take sideroads
not expecting much of anything
Looking the part isn't enough
Everyone is suspicious after
divisions within tribes, families, clans
I heard good advice, "find the right relatives"
I was very very lucky
I did.

(For the Harlow Girls)
Illinois is full of Indians. Nobody really knows this.

Photo: Family beadwork: Oglala Lakota artist Ellowyn Locke

some people never learn

In America, we put murderers on monuments
   We can't get rid of them
   The hate lingers like a rotting smell
   Many forget the Nazis were hung for their crimes
   So ghosts dance on their graves

safe numbers

While the strippers bars are full of drunks,
   support groups are full of lonely wives
   while their children play with drugs
   In an alley behind the school house
   You see their faces
   The pain they can't talk about,
   locked up
   In hurt, loss, disappointment
   Secret gardens in full bloom

Out of numbness
humans hide their secrets
But the face can't lie
No one can be that careful
Each of them runs from their feelings
Because pain hurts,
because it's work to change things,
Because we're not taught how
to recover from disappointment
So we become dead out of fear

If we dare, if we dare
The reward is great,
Fear's control disappears
Your heart opens
Air suddenly flows in and out
Like you wake from a nightmare

Almost too weak to walk
You're able to see the circus,
reliving safe numbers and situations

No one but you could break the spell
When the shell breaks
You're fragile like a newborn
You can't return to your old life
Because it doesn't fit anymore

It's more than OK to be sensitive, it's essential,
it is necessary. . .

(c) 2006/2019

strong as a willow

My youth disappeared
   under spell and dominion,
   too powerless, too mute, and
   too weak to protest

   Maid, cook, whore, little girl, daughter
   Necessary, I believed, so
   I disappeared into their idea
   of what I should be

   I read their desires as directions,
   like their force, yet somehow
   my illusion had to be protected
   with all my energy and faith

   I trusted I would be safe
   I told myself it was love
   that it was worth it
   I was wrong, I was as good as dead

   I was incapable of love
   to any degree
   There was no emotion
   Just a cold heart, cold soul, cold

   I found memories of a little princess
   whose father took his piece
   then a procession of narcissists
   who either betrayed or enslaved

   Yet even a slave is rewarded

Angels arrive, teachers, books
that open my world of silence
and give me voice

There is no worthless left
just a force and direction
There are beliefs that allow no weakness
and no men left to dominate desire

Now, as I choose,
I am safe within my own walls,
alive in my body, strong as a willow,
as wild, as free.

(c) 2010/19

shark tank

The tank is dark but you'll do it,
   dive in, find the opening.
   You can't see the danger ahead
   then you think you might die trying.
   You hear from some who didn't succeed
   But you heard from others who did
   So you tell yourself you can
   The risk is worth it.

   You dive deep into the blood red water
   You hear voices say you shouldn't
   Your mother's voice, your father's voice
   and you hear your own self-pity.
   Your body resists yet you advance through fear.
   But sharks and memories
   can't hold you back anymore
   Your body and mind focus
   on one purpose.
   You will open your eyes and swim.
   There is an opening, so you search in the darkness
   You find a narrow space,
   to the bottom, and you finally reach it.

   Memory is key to survival.
   You feel them behind and above you,
   You see the illusions that held you there.
   You see that you cannot stop ever again
   You see that you cannot go back
   or they will try and kill you all over again.
   And for that moment, you are finally sure
   As you shimmy through, and feel yourself floating

To the surface, to the light. . .
No risk has ever been so great as
having your own life. . .
Save yourself

© 2003/2019

porcupine gifts

It wasn't easy to find porcupine quills
   unless I found road kill
   in northern Wisconsin, my old stomping grounds,
   where I grew up.
   I kept an empty box in the trunk of my Chevy Impala,
   always on the lookout for porcupine.
   In 1981, my parents called to say they risked their lives
   on a curve on country trunk highway "T";
   I couldn't wait to see this granddaddy of porcupines
   (their words to describe him).
   They boxed him up for me, and left him behind
   their cabin, deep in the Wascott woods.
   On the drive north from the Twin Cities,
   I planned my harvest: leather gloves,
   thick towels, an old ice cream pail and a strong
   stomach for a smell
   I'd almost grown used to…
   Never a hunter, I was a gatherer:
   The American Indian Center in Minneapolis traded me
   seed beads for quills.

In those days, I was a rock singer,
making my own quill and peyote-stitch earrings.
My parents **had** found the granddaddy
with the finest thickest quills I'd ever seen.
I threw a towel on his big body and pressed down
wearing my leather gloves to harvest his quills
by pulling the towel up;
then towels would be stashed in a plastic bag
to prevent quill-poking accidents;
then I gave porcupine a proper burial.

Granddaddy easily gave me a thousand gifts.
I heard how the Anishinabe used pliant bark-paddles
tapping porcupine's back as he'd run away.
I heard some leave the barb on the quill
so it will penetrate
and not release from the bark when making
quill baskets.
No, I never wanted to chase a porcupine:
Tony's dogs in Porcupine, South Dakota,
had quills stuck clear through their snout.
Quills were real protection,
shot at predators like bullets.
Cleaning quills was the real trick
not getting stuck by the small sharp hooked barb
at the end of each quill;
I never went to an emergency room
though I got stuck plenty of times.
I pulled the barb out of my fingertips myself
and applied rubbing alcohol to my poked pads.
After I soaked the quills in water, I'd wipe them off
and clip off both ends with scissors,
sorting them into bags of lengths and thickness.
In the summer of 1983, a young bull-rider
brought me a traffic casualty so I could make him
a necklace of porcupine claws;
I was working with Craig at the Heart Six Dude Ranch
in Moran, Wyoming; he wore my necklace for protection
on dangerous rodeo bulls.
In the 90s, I sat in awe in the kitchen
of a Lakota quill artist in Pine Ridge
and watched as she'd soak the quill in her mouth
to soften it, then with grace she'd bend them
around metal hoops creating medicine wheels
from quills she'd dyed yellow, black, red and white,
colors of the four directions.
One of her medicine wheels hangs in my car
to protect me.

On a road trip in 2006,
I bought a small quilled birch bark basket in Ontario;
I would honor porcupine in my home
with this hand-crafted beauty by
talented Ojibwe quill artist Darlene Whitehead-Stevens.
I filled my little lidded basket with cedar and sage,
to attract good spirits and to honor porcupine
for his gift of protection.
Today there's a plastic tub filled with porcupine quills
in the back of my closet, stored with my bead supply.
Some quills are from granddaddy porcupine.
I'd never waste a gift so sacred.

© 2011

Quill Basket I bought in Ontario (my photo 2019)

tales of wisconsin...1

A stray bluebird, six white tail deer,
   Two bald eagles, an enormous grey owl
   here
   in Wisconsin
   on my last visit
   Mother has her stories
   About a less than shy wolf who met her gaze
   One Saturday afternoon
   And a mother badger and her pups
   Along the county road
   And one straggly coyote who really needed
   A good brushing and bath
   Or the herd of deer that came
   Thudding around the house
   like a pack of wild horses
   sometime last fall
   and the two black bears
   hanging out of Bobby's trees
   who figured out how to
   move the clothesline
   where his birdfeeders were hanging
   for safety
   One unlucky insect persists, Mother tells me,
   And it seems only bay leaves in the windows
   Will make the ladybugs leave
   Or prevent more from making
   The inside their home
   Mother's tales of Wisconsin, once my home...

tales of wisconsin...2

Wild Wisconsin
   Driving to and from the garbage dump
   three wild turkeys
   are on the roadside
   where a three-point buck
   stood the day before,
   this must be my lucky day.

   The best season is fall,
   with my car windows rolled down
   playing pow wow music
   going and coming:
   Live on WOJB
   in Lac Courte Oreilles
   so my emerald forest,
   golden trees and frisky deer can hear
   and remember
   the earlier inhabitants,
   my Anishinaabe friends
   and their sacred songs.

   (c) 2004

tales of wisconsin...3

Hummingbirds buzz
  dive for turf
  While Oreilles find the nectar
  And with fierce determination
  and song, the birds hop and swoop
  in and out of view,
  Eating quickly as they do.
  A young bald eagle readily takes his spot
  atop the dead white birch out front,
  with a clear view of shimmering Crystal Lake
  while a loon calls to his mate,
  traveling lake to lake.
  Frisky squirrels do acrobats,
  To avert becoming an eagle's snack.
  A Great Blue Heron calls this home,
  along the shore he lifts his long wings
  for a quieter territory
  as I had invaded his space near the shore. . .
  At this bird palace,
  Everyone is welcome here. . .
  A curious witness I become
  remote Wild Wisconsin
  winged ones find solace
  now that I've gone. . .

© 2004

birdsong

A small bird sang out to me
   In the concrete jungle
   As I walked the pavement, hot with heat
   And I wondered
   How did this bird survive,
   what did he eat?
   People were too busy to notice
   One tiny bird's song
   Rushing to their destination,
   Not feeling the beat under their feet
   They didn't even notice
   The rush in their pace
   Or the noise
   Or heavy air you could actually see
   Or the tiny bird.
   Still, at the hopelessness of the rush
   I heard the birdsong
   And I trembled for him,
   Perched high on the ledge
   Of a skyscraper
   where the trees are cropped and cut to fit,
   where tiny flowers spring up through the cracks
   In this man's world of concrete.
   But even here you can find
   A tiny bird singing
   Trying to remind us of our mother, the earth
   back in nature, under the trees,
   Along mighty lakes and streams,
   where we all belong. . .

© 1997 (Minneapolis, Minnesota)

31

funny?

It's funny
  How one minute
  You feel so alive,
  The next so afraid.
  One minute you're hurting
  One minute you're brave.
  Some would call this
  A personality disorder…
  That's not funny.
  © 1998

brain tricks (memory of a mouse)

I heard a quantum physicist say in an interview on NPR they planted memories in a mouse...and it worked...but how do they really know?

Memories are like brain-tricks:
    one-sided,
    lop-sided,
    funny,
    sad,
    selective,
    fickle,
    twisted,
    slanted,
    ruined,
    guilt-ridden,
    contaminated,
    contorted,
    despised,
    revised,
    regurgitated,
    treasured,
    profound,
    glorious,
    illustrated,
    light,
    dark,
    so what kind of memories will this mouse have?
(c) 2011

Big Media's power grab has sucked the life out of TV, and you and me. The viewer is the big loser. TV is for idiots now.

rebirth

Drug the sheep
  medicate their water
  They can
  hit us in the showers
  in our water fountains
  everywhere
  garbage in
  garbage out
  Stores of drugs
  dose everyone,
  even kids
  big bucks
  add tv buzz
  add computer terminal hypnosis
  add non-stop barrage of drug ads

Who are these monster drug giants
who are the dope sellers
We discover
Big Liars hide in their mansions
purified and silent
We'll sue them poor
so the Big People
will have to live in the same cesspool

The Earth will stop this madness
with one big push, rebirth,
rivers of blood

people waking up

People waking up then going to bed
   In front of a television,
   the nightmare,
   all of us walking zombies

   Flickers of flesh numb, forgetful, on a diet of fear
   People grow too paralyzed to shut down
   Big polluter and who they (s)elect
   If Uncle Sham spent a billion on energy, not bombing Iraq or
Syria or Afghanistan
   Maybe everyone would be free
   The People defeating
   fear Mother Earth will die soon
   The People walking
   get far away from TV chatter
   Ghosts greeting the few Indians
   Still hanging out in the woods

   It's Big
   This Guilt
   It's Big
   This Blame
   It's Big
   This Chatter.
   It's Big.
   It's Just a Big Game.

   © 2019 (revised from 2007)

Modern Medicine?

Modern-day Mengele's chose who they pierce, butcher, or torture
  ...we humans are their new Living Experiments,
  Using our bodies in medical trials, chemo-protocols,
  poisoned without impunity
  But call this modern marvels and miracle medicine,
  (this is not about healing but cold hard cash, **big big** bucks)
  They've lost their minds **and** the Hippocratic Oath...
  They capitalize on illness, disease, who to treat, who to kill.
  Drug companies, insurance moguls and hospital corporations,
  the people on their boards, profit from our loss;

  Human flesh they will sacrifice, so no one is truly safe...
  Getting starting, warming up on new victims
  of global drought and famine, they'll watch silently, patiently
  It's all a game to them... a game... the "reduce the population"
game...

  Many of us are victims of torture, mind control, adoption, ethnic
cleansing
  a vast conspiracy to reformat the poor child to zombie
  emotionally dead, grief-struck, paralyzed, stuck,
  shamed and ashamed, betrayed, demoralized
  There are many ways to destroy and hurt a human,
  many ways to torture and imprison, but let's call it "assimilate"
  Legal eugenics, all the while illegal, immoral...
  Madness warfare disguised as Third World diplomacy.

  In so many ways, lunatics are running the asylum,
  wearing white lab coats, military uniforms and business suits,
  who can't wait to think of new ways to torture us

bleeding us dry for money, gathering awards, recognition and
prestige...
    telling us all the while they're searching for the cure
    as they build their bank accounts, and kid's trust funds
    Mengele's Angels of Death simply spread to North and South
America,
    they who still reign... evil incarnate, are the Nazi curse on
mankind.

Here in America we starve on unhealthy food and corporate
greed,
    eating boxed and canned poison, tainted to toxic perfection
    brimming with sugar and fat, e coli, bacteria, fungus, and virus,
    It's not a matter of how we die
    but when...
    And any who challenge the angels of death
    are called mad, insane...
    © 7-24-2011

Josef Rudolf Mengele (March 16, 1911—February 7, 1979)
was a German SS officer and a physician in the Nazi concentration
camp Auschwitz-Birkenau. He earned doctorates in anthropology
from Munich University and in medicine from Frankfurt
University. He initially gained notoriety for being one of the SS
physicians who supervised the selection of arriving transports of
prisoners, determining who was to be killed and who was to be
a forced laborer, but is far more infamous for performing grisly
human experiments on camp inmates, including children, for
which Mengele was called the "Angel of Death". In 1940, he was
placed in the reserve medical corps. In 1942, he was wounded at
the Soviet front and pronounced medically unfit for combat, then
promoted to the rank of SS-Captain for saving the lives of three
German soldiers. He survived the war, and after a period living
incognito in Germany he fled to South America, where he evaded
capture for the rest of his life despite being hunted as a Nazi war
criminal.

FOOTNOTE: http://en.wikipedia.org/wiki/Josef_Mengele

mommy

Mothers who felt unloved, discarded
  withheld love.
   My love wasn't for them enough.
   That made me sensitive, fragile, bullied.
   This pain would force me to look deep.
   I must love myself.
   Mommy, hold me. Don't leave me now.
   Don't you love me?
   Did I do something?
   There was no answer.

We are the sum of our ancestors.

the whore is home

Bobby told me a story.
He remembered when we first met.
When I got to the house,
dad said "the whore is home."
And Bobby told me he felt sick, shocked that a father could
say something like that about his own daughter.
But I wasn't his daughter. I was his whore, not his biological
daughter.
I am the one he molested, the one he terrified, the one he cursed.
I told Bobby I had to be the bigger person.
I had to be strong. I had no choice.
Christ was a good teacher.
It makes me wonder now,
how did I survive?
How did I?

hurt

NO NO NO
   You cannot hurt me
   because I **know** you
   your heart and your actions
   are your own
   you cannot betray me again
   I have been aware of you a long time
   a long time, and I watched
   as you struggled
   never at peace
   Stealing from me now,
   then lying about it,
   justifying it,
   that is no longer something I tolerate.

   You are not my relative or my brother.
   You never were.

child (song lyrics)

Child
    Conspiracy of silence
    Every story in you hides,
    surprise
    Silent to the end,
    No one knows what makes you cry
    Trauma of a child
    Running from the past. At last
    Shadows hiding in the dark
    The mind wounds fast, Child

    Fears of what it will do to you
    Scars underneath the skin
    Secure in knowing you'll move on
    Starting over, settling in
    Abused neglected lonely soul
    Bitter mystery, Child

    Not forgotten… lonely child
    Run, run, running on, running wild
    Broken will, broken dreams
    Sacrificed children, silent screams
    Ohhhhhhh, child

Song lyrics I wrote about Kim Peterson, for my band
"Sardaukar" in Kennewick, WA ©February 1980

race (song lyrics)

Old men with change in their pockets,
   young people who won't even try,
   The trouble with being happy
   Is you could look until you die.

   The life we have is so short
   Busy people soon forget
   An existence based on money
   is never a sure bet…

   I can't believe the hurry
   Or the race to get ahead
   The harder we try to succeed
   The easier we're lead

   What you really want to have
   won't pop up if you search
   You can't start life at the altar
   when you meet your bride at the church

   Our world will keep on turning
   The soap opera will never die
   You've got to keep returning
   By the next show you'll know why

   I can't believe the hurry
   Or the race to get ahead
   The harder we try to succeed
   The easier we're lead,
   Yeah it's real easy to be dead.

The moral of this story
Is some things will never change
The minute you try counting
The rhythm ain't the same…
No, the rhythm ain't the same…

(c) 1980 SARDAUKAR song lyrics

tell me (song lyrics)

Times before
   When things went well
   Giving everything you could,
   You would…

   Tell me
   All the things you feel
   Tell me
   How much is it real
   Tell me
   Everything you can
   Tell me
   I can understand

   Others take so much of you
   All your promises and plans, all they can…

   Tell me
   All the things you feel
   Tell me
   How much can they steal
   Tell me
   All the things you do
   Tell me
   What you're going through

   How much can you really mean
   Being forced again to choose, to lose…

   Tell me
   All the things you feel

Tell me
How much of it's real
Tell me
Everything you can
Tell me
I can understand

heart-shaped ass

(my beauty in pounds)

They capture us with their beauty,
their air-brushed radiance.
Beauty still wears a tiny bikini
big breasts, tiny waist, fake tan …
smiling, anorexic, hopeful.
Her brand of pretty could earn millions,
make her a trophy, a pin-up,
a Farrah-Paris somebody.
Somehow beauty convinces us
we're just not pretty enough
or thin enough
or even worth mentioning.
Her images glitter everywhere …
TV, print ads, Billboards.
A million times we see
beauty matters.

Invited to the Christmas dance in junior high
I feel extra extra beauty because
my parents spend an entire paycheck
on the velvet dress with gold brocade
and bell-shaped sleeves.
Rob, student council president, asked my strict parents
who approved since he's a lawyer's son.
Marathon dancing with the president
I decide I'll run for student council.
Elected vice president, we both make the local newspaper.

I choose to be smart. Beautifully smart.
I drop 30 pounds before high school.
Mom dyes my mousey brown locks to blonde when I am 16.
I tell my parents I'm going to college
and they say we can't afford it,
So I tell my grandmother
and she says you have to go,
despite what they say.
I figure out the financial aid forms, get accepted,
start college in high school and live on a budget.
I can survive a whole day on a bag of potato chips.

In college I can be different, not perfect.
To be strong, act strong,
even when *confident* feels weird, Grandma says.
My body still doesn't fit the magazine images
so I lose 20 pounds on a high protein diet.
I run for College Homecoming Queen and win.
A fraternity makes me little sister.
Dating two guys, I know I'll marry neither one.

Many many girls still intimidate me,
their beauty, their rich parents,
but they just don't bother me as much.
I want my degree in three years instead of four,
Grandma approves but passes away before I graduate.
The women in my course, Counseling Women,
say women don't need makeup, bras, or high heels
to make it in this world.
Mom still likes me better in a dress,
makeup on, hair perfect,
and she buys me new clothes
for church, for subtle inspiration.
Goodwill clothes are ghetto.
Mom believes beauty is necessary
to be successful, to get noticed, to get a husband.

After all the magazines, blow dryers, bad perms,
I'm still not the Vogue vision of beauty,
not even after one meal a day and yoga class
one wealthy cousin in Illinois recommends.
I drop 25 pounds for a beauty pageant my college senior year.
The college guy who looked so disinterested
is now totally interested in this body.
We live together, and he watches my weight for me.
I can't seem to get rid of him and move 10 states away.

At 27, I marry a millionaire for security,
But this guy demands his trophy wife stop smoking.
Eating past my fear and paranoia,
I gain 60 pounds in just 6 months
then spend 10 years on a treadmill
and exercise bike to drop 10 pounds.
I decide the only way to feel better is drop the guy …

It takes 10 years to find the courage.
Beauty took a backseat.
At 48, after 48 unsuccessful diets, grey hair since 28,
my new husband, my Black Indian from Harlem,
loves me
and reminds me to eat.
My heart-shaped ass refuses to be camouflaged.
Even though I am no longer mannequin perfect
But a healthy size 16
Finally freely brilliantly
I feel full of beauty.

© 2012 (revised from 2005)

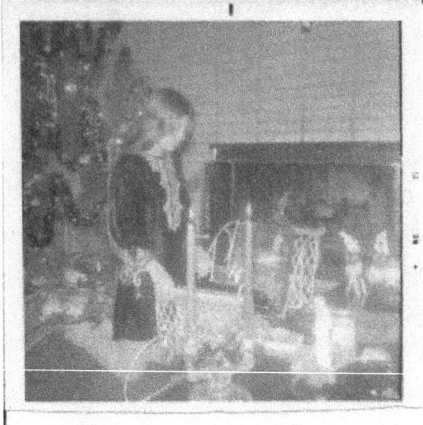

that velvet dress I still have

This poem was published in Yellow Medicine Review, Spring 2008 and in the anthology I WAS INDIAN (Vol. 2) 2012 (Susan Deer Cloud, editor)

PART DEUX My Beauty in Pounds

(Part 2) My beauty in pounds/Heart-Shaped Ass ::: a prose-in-progress about my beauty disorder "[1]"

I'm hoping to get some idea
how you're supposed to act
and feel as a late teen
because the magazine cover
said you'd get the guy
looking hot, gorgeous
and so I read everything twice.
Then one day I meet him,
the cutest guy who
smells so good, acts so arrogant,
stupidly he convinces me
how his sex is for love and
our sex is definitely LOVE.
So I do it and I'm sore
and I wonder if I was OK
if he liked me
I act like it felt good
but somehow it didn't.
So after reading more Cosmo
I talk with a girlfriend who also
had sex and never told her parents.
We can't agree how sex is supposed to feel.

That guy moves on to his next,
and I decide in the bathroom mirror
that I wasn't so bad, so

1. beauty disorder

53

I convince myself I'll try again.
Maybe I can get a new guy
if I have the right information.
*

The plan fails
I still don't feel or look like
sexy models in the magazines.
I feel average. I'm a rock singer.
I buy hair color, makeup, rouge,
lip gloss, mascara, Visine
and hope it will be enough
until a friend from an acting class says
I don't wear any make-up.
Adding more make-up doesn't
go over with the parents who say
I'm looking more like the girl from the
wrong side of the tracks, not
the girl-next-door.
Guys do notice and try
demeaning remarks yet
their pick-up lines fail on me.
*

One musician says I lost weight, much better,
so my eating disorder kicks in to full-blast
speed keeps me going until 2 am
and thin.
*

Make-up doesn't make anyone as beautiful
as the pin-up girls in gas station calendars.
A haircut and perm are not exactly
what I had in mind but try anyway
then spend a paycheck on straightener and gel
and it takes an hour to get ready for anything.

Really attractive girls seem happier
with new clothes, convertibles,
confident with boyfriends

I see them party on Lake Minnetonka
their dads are lawyers, doctors, rich.
Everyone seems better than me
I try harder to look better
try tighter clothes
try new make-up
try blonder
but I'm still not Biffy or Muffy

One friend in Minneapolis
takes her clothes off for Playboy
but finds out she's rejected
her breasts were too small.
We decide rich girls buy new boobs
but won't graduate on their GPA
or find a good mate
if you're naked
in a magazine.
We fail ourselves, both of us adoptees.
*
I fail miserably.
I imagine marriage is better
because he gets you, understands you,
because he loves you
I'll probably enjoy the sex
and figure out why everyone is doing it
and making it sound so great.
It has to get better.
But it doesn't.
I don't marry until I'm 27,
he's 18 years older.
Sex is everything
I'm a trophy.
I'm no better than a prostitute.

*Beauty Disorder? This story and this world is a work in

progress. I am a work in progress. You are a work in progress. Believe me.

I have an eating disorder. I have ideas, diets, doctors. Why? It's an unhealthy sick world that makes us sick.

I had cancer surgery in May 2018. I'd done tons of research, and KNOW THE CAUSE [https://knowthecause.com]

seattle

Seattle, Washington

I love Seattle. I miss Seattle. A few years ago I wrote about band clothes on my LARA blog.

Years ago I had a conversation in Seattle with a musician who told me, *"**music is medicine**."* He even had a small record label by that name.

Music **was** my focus and life in my teens and 20s. I was a professional rock musician. It was more than a career. It was a calling… (and the weird thing is I am not finding any people in my first family who had musical talent but both my adoptive parents were both talented musicians.)

I'd kept quite a few "vintage" dresses from my rock band days, which was in my 20s, eons ago. They are kinda like a scrapbook of fabrics (yet I don't sew a lick!)

Why do I keep them? …these are many many good reasons…

First, I am from a family of dressy women. My adoptive mom Edie wore evening gowns! I can't even imagine a holiday dinner when she and I (and guests) weren't dressing up. When I left home at age 17 I had little money to buy like her but I did collect a mix of vintage rayon, satin, silk and retro velvet.

Second, when you are in a rock band, you barely make rent money. Wearing unusual band clothes was a "fitting" thing to do... especially if you are female. Fitting is my way of telling you it was very hard for me to afford tailoring. The rock bands I joined had no budget, seamstresses, or dress codes. When I started in the late 70s, there were a tiny handful of female singers. ((Hint: Linda Ronstadt was one. Heart came along eventually.))

Third, most of these dresses were found in thrift stores yet they are probably the most precious creations I could own or wear. One vintage 1940s black rayon midi-length has two beaded hummingbirds. I also wore this to work in Seattle, I wore it to nightclubs, I wore it on a cruise. It is still lovely but I did a crappy job hemming it years ago...I found a tiny hole in the bottom of the dress. (No tag inside means it must have been handmade.)

Fourth, mainly it's the feel of fabric and touching recreates memory for me. (Sometimes I think being adopted did cause me some brain damage and trapped some memory in fog.) (I've kept some old tshirts from my travels too; some are from bands, of course.)

I think of band clothes as body armor; in a way these simple clothes create an illusion that isn't there. Black leather pants — and what do you think?

Some of my rock band clothes were gifted. One blue velvet dress was given to me in college by a classmate (the mother of Wendy who I knew somewhat in high school). Her mom wanted **me** to have this family heirloom and of course I did wear it often. (I do wonder if Wendy knew about this?)

There is even a pink quilted bed jacket my mom gave me. No, I have not worn it. When did the bed jacket thing get popular? I think women in the 1930s and 40s had much better "taste" than we do now. (I'll admit I've a taste for kitschy colorful table linens, too.)

The rayon green print wrap dress was found in an abandoned house in Wisconsin (my friend's grandmother lived there and was deceased) (I scooped up a black fur coat, too.) That green number was what I was wearing when I met Blackfoot. (You will have to read my memoir One Small Sacrifice to know that rock and roll saga). I also wore it when I sang in Automatic and then Tropic Zone in Minneapolis.

I didn't give up on music; my first marriage killed it for me.

drowning

When we married,
I told him to let go,
stop trying to swim upstream
All he had to do was let go and let the current take him
    But he fought fate,
he fought me, he fought life, he thought if he fought
hard enough, long enough, people would change,
he'd change them, change me.
    All stubbornness and ego, he forgot past lives,
drowning then, drowning now,
drowning over and over again
If time froze, he'd push it back, start fresh
    He told the story of drowning to anyone who would listen:
a boy without clothes, without permission to swim,
the river sweeping him up, his grandmother's frightened face,
dying, the white light, an older boy finally pulling him out,
saving him.
    When he saw the light, it wasn't his time
No matter how many times he told it,
he still didn't give up his thirst for power, position, prestige,
more power
    The river tried…
(for Dave)

Published in Rabbit and Rose 2014
Lake Oswego, Oregon
Many years ago, 01984 actually, I read an interesting article
in Cosmopolitan magazine about healers. I was living in Oregon
and engaged to be married. Dave proposed to me on Friday the
13, that July. We decided to get married on Crystal Lake at my
parents retirement home in Wascott, WI, and the Larrabee siblings

were set to meet there for a family reunion, too. When I got to Wisconsin, my adoptive dad Everett was sick. Throwing up sick. Taking him to doctors was my new job, like an ambulance driver. It was during surgery on August 3, the doctors said cancer and gave him 6 months. On August 4th, the wedding happened, many people flew in, lots of lovely gifts, a big meal, but it's still a blur to me. We drove north to Duluth in our wedding clothes to see my dad in the hospital, since he was unable to walk me down the sidewalk/aisle.

When I got back to Lake Oswego, Oregon, I wrote letters to the healers in that Cosmo article. One of them was Patricia Sun, in California. She mailed me a cassette tape. Patricia was known for making a sound, a mysterious sound, deep from inside her. It resonated in every one who heard it.

Since dad wasn't interested in healers or thinking outside the western medicine paradigm, healing spirit wasn't in the realm of possibility for him, sadly.

Everett died exactly six months later on April 3, 1985.

I had my own ideas then about healing and my thoughts have matured as I have.

Take a listen to Patricia Sun's work. (There are more videos of her on youtube, of course.)

My first husband David Seitzinger died in 2006. Obit

you broke me

I didn't think I'd ever be able to see
    that far back…
    Lack courage? Who, Me?
    How could I ever look back at those years
    With any kind of perspective?
    Especially when I was
    so sick,
    so split
    so confused,
    so hurt,
    so abandoned,
    So alone, so abused, so manipulated, so aghast at every turn, so naïve, so fucking stupid, so fucking manipulated, so disappointed, so broken, so twisted
    So rushed, so played to, so lied to, so lied to…
    I never knew it was a giant manipulation (not back then)

    I didn't even realize he was still having an affair with Char
    He told me once I'd never know if he cheated on me,
    I didn't know… I really didn't.
    I'm glad I kept the journals.
    That life is over now. I can burn them now with those memories.
    It's true that people settle for things. I chose chaos. I settled badly.
    I got the lesson plan.
    Was it karma?
    Trophy wife bitterness? Absolutely not.
    I'll never have to relive that again.

    "Magic is we believe so little of what is real and in front of us."

faces

Look at your face very close
Every mark crevice worry-line wrinkle bump
Try different light, in a mirror, in the sun
Take your time
Just look at your eyes now, their color
What are they saying
What are they saying **to** you
Are they asking for anything?
Are your eyes telling you to be nicer to yourself?
Are your eyes angry or kind?
Now look at your skin
What makes it better or different
What makes you better or different
Does the tone and texture make you proud, happy, uneasy
Does a freckle or mole remind you of something
Do you wear a scar from chicken pox or an accident
Do you have more than one scar
Do you remember when you got them and how
Now imagine your eyes are only visible
How does wearing a skin suit make you feel?
© 2013

swimmers

There are no pool rules for lunatics and love.
    Lunatics who seek to bring everyone else
    to the same end, I swim faster faster faster to escape
    to breathe. I'm not alone.
    Many were in my same boat.
    Some drowned, some made it to shore, some went missing,
    Some struggled with sanity, too.
    I just want to bury my head in my mother's neck.
    We remember things we never should have seen.
    People derailed,
    unhinged by other's cruelties.
    Those that didn't recover bring scars to me.
    I barely manage to save myself
    but a few swimmers I heal
    with a rule of love.
    © 2012

jump

J
    .....U
    ....M
    . . . . .P

I jump with evolution
As a child of the stars,
a witness to human frailty
I study the masters,
Mystics, prophets, poets
to absorb their magic
I propel mountains of knowledge
But fall back, poisoned by pollution
Broken by my own ignorance and innocence
My blood stores so many memories
every horrific mistake, every genocide,
Things I would just as soon forget.

So I pray myself well.

(c) 2010

swallow manifesto

To our population:

 We do not recognize laws, divisions, fences, borders, countries, counties, states, presidents, governors, police, park rangers, scientists, paramilitary or queens…

 We are neither citizens or immigrants,

 pagan or christian, wild or captive,

 sinner or saint, active or inactive, atheist or evangelical,

 democrat or republican, conservative or liberal, socialist or communist

 American or Canadian, right wing or left wing, red state or blue state

 Fettered or unfettered, safe or unsafe, foreigner or local

 Sane or insane, balanced or imbalanced, pure or impure,

 Insider or outsider, modest or immodest, moral or immoral.

 Human labels:

 misfits, holy, dangerous, judged, colonized,

 controlled, saved, enslaved, damned and condemned.

Your orders: Migrate. Fly.

See "About the Poet" for more on this poem

too much to change

...It seems there is too much to change
We think it is still safe to teach our children the ways we were
taught
but it's not
There is too much to change
We have grown too familiar
with oppression, inequality
There is not much to hope for
where nothing is sacred
I wish we could forget everything
Instead of fear
we'd practice acceptance
of every child and ancestry
We would sing songs
to the trees and animals
We would grow a big garden buzzing with insects
and stop all polluters and their pollution
Instead of giving gifts, we'd give attention
We would be involved with freedom for all
and create a safe place to grow old

People would work at what they love,
no longer slaves to money and taxes
using their gifts of creativity,
not in a race or competition

We will not learn to change until we look at history,
until we become less numbed, dazed,
until we become more aware of our need to feel safe
There will be no change
until we change our perspective,

restore innocence,
until we all try harder.

**"People change for two main reasons:
either their minds have been opened or
their hearts have been broken" –Steven Aitchison**

my heart (for wildcat)

Married 15 years (in 2019), but you say 20
   you really are my frog prince
   I asked for a sign
   I got you

   It's not about me honey bunny
   but the choices we make.
   I cannot save you
   from your history or mine. . .
   I cannot change it.
   In every moment
   I feel less alone, less hurt, but not safe.
   (no one is ever truly safe)

   Somehow, I believe you are here
   To give me the message
   "love will sustain us"
   You approach, you dare to walk further
   You fill me and empty me
   You challenge me and you solve me
   You desire as I desire
   You saved me from my self.

   You sat and listened
   as I sat speechless

   I know you will not hurt me
   You will only torture yourself
   with more questions
   that I have no answers for. . .

A tiger cannot change his stripes
And you cannot help who we are.

Did I jump too far?
My heart says yes. . .
and I am so happy.
© 2004/2019

you complete me

Women are like trees,
   Growing faithfully
   Minute by minute, thought by thought
   Securely rooted in the earth
   Arms reaching to the heavens
   Twisting and bending to follow the sun...

   Men are like Birds
   Fluttering at first
   Then practicing maneuvers
   Until one day love calls
   And the Bird lands
   Choosing one Tree to build a life upon...

   Tree welcomes Bird,
   bright with his feathers and fancy talk,
   while he learns to accept his new position
   with a view from Tree's highest branch.
   Bird grows strong
   while Tree whispers her secrets
   carried on the breeze,
   "You complete me,
   You complete me."

(c) 1998

what i know

The open heart remains a sacred mystery
　　As wisdom grows,
　　the greatest love delivers hope
　　That is what we know

　　All around us, lovers get tangled and twisted
　　Human nature so brutal and obsessive
　　And fear so instinctual
　　That is what we know.

　　Long ago a monster changed me
　　In one moment crushing my heart in his hands
　　I learned then if I fear, I can't love
　　That is what I needed to know.

　　Love lessens pain, washes away sadness
　　And massages the contours of memory
　　Love can heal anyone
　　That is what I wanted to know.

　　Love can end a child's curse
　　Love can move a lover to fight a monster
　　And win.
　　That is what I know.

　　As sacred a mystery, love is the cure
　　The medicine, the magic,
　　The sword and the savior
　　Love is what I know.

© 2012 (revised from 1990)

earth tribes at the millennium (essay)

Trace L Hentz

> This was written so long ago, maybe 1995. I'd made a very early website as a test (in 2000) and flowed an earlier longer version of Earth Tribes I'd drafted. My vision was to have a actor Floyd Red Crow Westerman (Dances with Wolves) read it aloud. (This was long before ebooks and youtube).

Not long ago, I woke hearing a voice; it was not the first time. I dutifully got up and went to the notebook I write in every morning. I call it the voice of my ancestors.

Then I realized this message wasn't for me only. To see life from a new view, like an eagle, looking down from the stars, the message is quite simple. Very.

The message is for the new millennium.

We grow and learn that the Earth is abundant, green and full of living things. Trees are covered with fruit and gardens are full of fresh vegetables. The blue lakes and rivers are her blood vessels, winding and weaving all over the land supplying water to drink. The mountains gather snow for the spring's thaw, replenishing the rivers again and again. The minerals from the mountain make the water taste good and soil rich and dark. When a mountain erupts, the ash is sent by the four winds, also making the soil more fertile. The trees breathe and make the air clean and fresh again. It is a cycle, never ending.

We feel the air, water and land are each connected. The layer of air above the earth provides protection from the sun's heat. There are ice caps at both ends of the orb to keep the weather in the middle mild. We have four seasons of renewal. Everything has a purpose to make the earth live-able. The earth and its creatures are a complex world of interdependent parts.

The tribes lived in groups, called nations. The people speak many different languages. Some tribes conquer other tribes. Some rule with terror and some with peace. Each earth tribe wants to protect itself. It has a chief and warriors to do that. And they protect the inventions and food supply. Most have a medicine man to treat its sick called doctors and guards they call police. The young are sent to school, they learn to read & write if they are lucky.

When the young are done with school in 12 or 16 years, they work in factories to buy land and houses. They also buy their own transportation. Once we rode horses, now it is a gas-powered motorcar.

There are all kinds of tribes: yellow, black, brown, red and white. Some think because of that they are different from the rest. Some even think they are better than the others. So most tribes decide to keep separate, not mix and not like each other. They build fences or have drawings of their lands called maps.

Some colors were almost erased. Millions and millions of the red tribe died when the white tribe arrived to start a new nation. The black tribe was taken in chains to work for the white man there. The white man exploded a mushroom cloud over the yellow tribe. One tribe across the great ocean had a ruler who put thousands of people in ovens to die because he wanted their riches and didn't like their beliefs.

What tribe will ever completely rule the earth is still undecided. Because they do not choose to accept each other, they feel one must be better and dominate the rest.

There are young men and women of all colors who watch a small box of moving pictures called a television. They get their ideas from it. One girl won't eat and her mother takes her to a doctor who says she has an eating disorder called anorexia. They put her in a hospital but the girl still thinks she is fat and starves herself to death. A young boy takes a gun to school and shoots his classmate after they argue on the playground. He takes the gun from his father's house.

In some places, people make up stories and they are made into a moving picture. They hire people to say and act the words and tape it with a camera and play it on a big screen or on the television. They use a lot of money, the people who say the words and the people who tell them how to say it. The story is called a movie.

There aren't many tribes who spend time with their children anymore. Some young are sent to live at school or and some go to an institution if they act angry. Some children run away to live on the streets and not in their parents houses. Some children get lots of presents but never see their parents. Some children decide to steal things and some make themselves dizzy and dull with drugs and alcohol. Some even commit suicide.

Some children are not wanted by their parents. They are taken away by a judge and sent to live with others. The people who hurt or molest the young ones are caught more now because the children tell their secrets. The guilty are sent to a place with iron bars called prison. Each tribe has its own way to judge the bad.

There are women in every tribe now who leave home to go to work. They do not watch over their children but pay someone else to do it. Some mothers get money from the father of the children, if they are not together. Some men get arrested and put behind iron bars if they don't pay. One nation collects a tax from everyone to pay for mothers and children and they call it 'welfare'. Most tribes have a system to provide for the elderly, sick, widows, orphans or unemployed.

In every tribe I know there is a ceremony called marriage. A man and women make a promise 'to love and honor, until death us do part'. Many do not keep that promise. Many do not know each other very well when they marry. This is hard on everyone. Their children get shared and shipped from house to house. Some have more than one mother and father and call them stepparents.

Some tribes are violent. There is rape of women and children. Some have robbers or serial killers who commit more than one murder. Doctors study them and write theories about why they are so sick.

Police guard and protect their tribe and catch the bad ones but not all are honest. Some bad ones hire a lawyer to defend them and explain their problems. They go in front of a jury of 12 people. The jury decides on guilt or innocence and the judge gives a punishment. Some tribes require you prove your innocence, others treat you as innocent until you are proved guilty. Some tribes give capital punishment where you are sentenced to die. Sometimes innocent die and sometimes guilty are set free.

There are gangs in the concrete jungles we call cities. Gangs wear suits or colors and carry guns and knives. They mean to protect their own and make money in stealing, slavery, weapons and drugs. Some of these men call their gang the Mafia or the Family. Young black men call their tribe Bloods or Crips.

There are some children who grow up in the concrete cities who don't see the forests or mountains, except on the picture box. They don't swim in lakes or see flowers bloom in the spring. They don't build snowmen or jump in autumn leaves. They live in the small rooms of an apartment and go to a crowded room at school to learn their lessons. Some play games called sports and never learn to read a book.

Because there are so many people, each tribe needs to choose a leader. In some they choose a President. The men who tell him what to think are called senators or representatives. That causes problems sometimes because big companies pay these senators money and tell them how to vote. The people choose sides and call them parties. Some leaders and presidents give permission to these big companies to do things that hurt their people but make money. Some companies make terrible poisons that hurt the water or make the air dark with smoke. Some make powerful weapons that are dangerous.

~

Many groups and tribes for centuries have argued over their land and boundaries which often start a war. Each tribe has an army, most of them men and they live in forts called stations or bases. They train them to fly air planes or steer ships. They learn to shoot guns and march. There is a man called a General who commands the big army. When one tribe gets angry enough, they declare war on each other. The war parties shoot at each other until they all die or someone calls a truce. Some armies are sent to a different country to fight with another army to win over the other warriors. They call them world wars. One time, they poisoned the air with a gas that killed many men in the other army. The yellow tribe dropped bombs on a navy base. Some tribes never fight, if they are lucky.

~

Some people get mad at their own tribe over what to pray about. They build a place to meet and call it a church. They write their own rules, or commandments, and call it their religion. Some churches tell their people what words to pray, what to think, how to act and make them follow their rules. Sometimes they say that the other churches are wrong. Then the churches collect money to build more churches. Some send people door to door to get people to join or some go on the television so you don't have to leave your house. Churches buy land and things then they become richer than others. Some send their people on a mission to another country. Churches have problems because some of their leaders have gone against their rules they call vows. Some leaders have sex when they promised not to. Some get too drunk on alcohol or give their people bad advice. Some leaders get caught taking money for themselves and get put behind the iron bars. One church was called a cult and it got burned to the ground with all the people in it. Another church has members who wear a white hood and burn crosses in the grass.

Under many stars and for many moons, some tribes made only the men leaders to rule over the others. Women didn't get to speak or vote. Women in one tribe had their feet wrapped in bandages so tight their feet grew wrong and twisted. Some women were not sent to school. Some babies were taken away and killed if they were girls. Some women were made sterile by surgery so they would not have babies, without their permission. One church said women will not be allowed into heaven unless they are married and have male children. Some churches called women witches and burned them to death.

~

Some tribes have invented things and make them in secret. Some trade goods with others across the great waterways, called oceans. Each wants to keep its invention or war machines a secret. But some tribes send spies to see what the other is doing. One country calls their spies the Central Intelligence Agency. Some spies get caught and put behind the iron bars because it is called treason to give away a secret. When tribes become friends, they are called allies so they share secrets and store weapons for each other. There is a group of tribes that maintain peace called the United Nations but not all tribes honor their peace pact and join. Some tribes have made promises called treaties.

~

There is disease for many tribes now. Some say it is because there is too much bad air and water. Tribes have medicine and hospitals for the sick. Some study sickness and make machines to look inside the body. The red tribe watched the animals, like bear, eat plants when they were sick and used the same plants to cure its people. Those doctors were called medicine men. Some tribes that have money are looking for a cure for the cancer and the new virus strains that kill so many.

Many think of our planet as an endless supply of food, minerals, plant life and animals yet many inventions are destroying this supply. Some concrete cities are overpopulated. Some nations are unable to feed everyone or give everyone a place to sleep. Some factories leak poisons into the air, water and land. Some farms spray poison on their crops to kill insects and supply us with this food. Some animals are fed things to grow big and fat and we eat those animals.

~

In some lands, there are kings and queens, in others, an emperor. Some rulers are called governors and mayors. Some groups are called Congress and another Parliament. These groups of government make new rules called laws and collect money they call tax. Some leaders don't follow the laws and have been fired for doing wrong or get overthrown by other governments.

There are more women leaders now. They grew tired of not being understood. They want the same pay as men in the factories. Some women are no longer prostitutes and slaves. Some say a woman will be a President in America very soon.

Some churches have closed because of bad leaders. Some factories are punished and fined for their pollution and waste. Some people who don't agree with the laws hold gatherings called rallies. One group of young people called 'hippies' marched and protested a war saying 'make love, not war.'

Many tribes are seeing that they are not so different from the rest. Some offer their hand in peace. Some are protecting women and children. Some are protecting animals from extinction. Some are protecting forests. Some food is being grown without the use of chemicals and sprays. Some are calling off the war and reducing their armies.

My red grandfather learned from his grandfather that all children need to be protected. Their decisions would affect many to come. Children in the red tribe were attended to by parents, close relatives, grandparents and elders. The red tribe raised all the children the same so they would grow strong and learn to be generous, not jealous and weak. They were good parents so the next generation would be. Our Chief took food to the starving or sick and gave them a place to sleep. We had no prison. The Chief was chosen because he was generous. He gave away many belongings in thanks for all that he received or for his dead relatives. We believe we are all related. Everything on earth is connected.

When we begin to see our sameness, we end our differences. When we accept peace, the children are happy. They will know how to care for themselves and others. They will know how to handle their anger without a weapon or war machine.

Acceptance of killing must end. When we all learn this lesson, there will be no more war.

~

It's Not Supposed to Be Like This

We are awakening...

This tale is about the "haves" and "have nots."

We've all heard campaign promises and political sermons, then once elected, we might catch a glimpse of the leader on TV and it appears all those promises are long gone, long forgotten. And why we elected them, those reasons are forgotten too.

It makes us angry we can't elect good leaders but then apathy sets in. We ask, what can **we** do? We're not as powerful as them.

We still wonder, "What happens to our chosen leaders?"

We see all the problems they need to fix: global poverty, low wages, high taxes, epic pollution, insanity like the BP Oil Spill, nukes like Japan's disaster Fukushima, Prison Corporation's enslavers, Bad Banksters who never go to jail, war upon war upon war, the exploitation and suffering of Trafficked Humans and the list goes on and on and on…

Our attention span is under three minutes now. TV transformed us into zombies. We might hear scary things prior to elections that surprise us, but by then it's too late. It's like we can't fix anything since these problems are too big for anyone to fix. That is just an illusion. We forgive our chosen leaders so easily.

Yet they keep us poor, in the dark, struggling, afraid. Leaders, who many call the elite, become unavailable, unreachable. They control us with promises and TV speeches. Nothing changes.

Human suffering has only grown. Division? It's their playbook. It's always between the haves and the have nots.

As gas and fuel prices inch higher and higher, I know someone is controlling prices to control us. Once gas prices reach a certain point, some of us will have to choose fuel or food. We know we have to choose our leaders better the next election but the cycle repeats itself over and over.

It seems our leaders lack empathy, like they have a brain virus and can't tell us the truth. It's like being elected gives them amnesia and all they want is to be reelected. And the cycle repeats while we wait for progress and change.

The elite feed off of us and our suffering. Whoever invented linear time did this to enslave us. Watching the clock, we become obsessed with the hours we work and the hours we watch TV. I read Matthew Fox's book, "The Reinvention of Work." Changing our workday to 30 hours could change the world! It would free us up to be parents and grandparents and not slaves to their system.

We fill stadiums to watch sports but we can't seem to gather enough people to end human slavery and suffering as it exists today.

Why is that?

Once **you** see the truth, you can't unsee it! I only ask that **you** ask questions to be awake.

(c) 2019

01010101

WHIM

I have been processing so long (60+ years) I kinda forget that trauma caused a dis/associative disorder I still have—and I do catch myself pretty fast if I seem to fall into the old mindset. Does anyone else realize that being adopted by strangers is mind-altering? (Perhaps that is why cruelty and torture has been used for centuries.)

Following my whim, I make folders on my computer for named projects for all the different "me's" —and when it's time I try and make them into something in a word document. No judgement—I just do it. This works for me: Follow your WHIM. Follow whatever the whim tells you—make art, create something. Don't judge yourself. Yeah, it's hard. Try harder.

Layers of Time

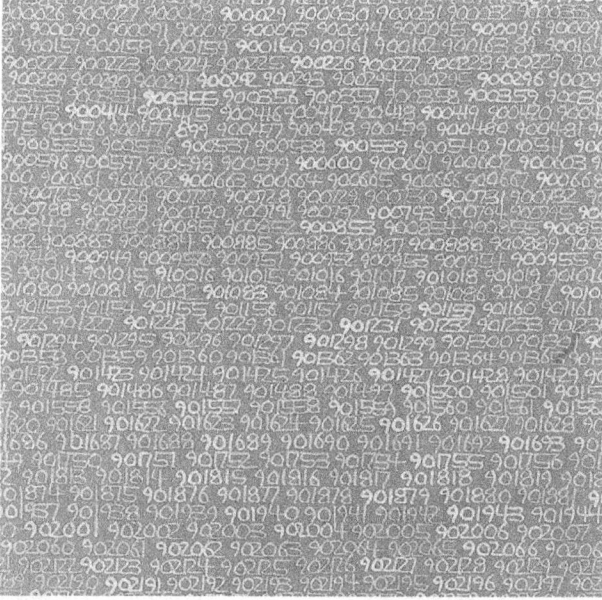

In 1965, artist Roman Opałka began painting 'time' from 1 to infinity. As he progressed, each canvas was lightened 1%, resulting in purely white-on-white pieces by 2007. The final number Opałka painted was on August 6, 2011, the day of his death: 5607249.

We are not bad timing… we chose this and we wanted to be here… right now…right here. We want to see this…

The Hopi have a saying "now is the time, we are the ones we have been waiting for…" Read it again: The Hopi have a saying "**NOW** is the time, **WE** are the ones we have been waiting for…" Trust Your INTUITION. This is not a mistake. We're balancing many lifetimes.

A new abnormal: It is *still* two minutes to midnight

No matter how we use our eyes, we still need to use our hearts to decide everything we do. —Trace Lara Hentz

IMAGINE, IF YOU WILL, THE PLANET AWAKENING & EXPERIENCING A SHIFT OF CONSCIOUSNESS SO GREAT

THAT GOVERNMENTS AROUND THE WORLD CONDUCT PSYCHOLOGICAL WARFARE ON THEIR OWN CITIZENS IN AN ATTEMPT TO CONTROL THEM BY LOWERING THEIR VIBRATIONS & KEEPING THEM IN A CONSTANT STATE OF FEAR.

Since the election in November 02016 and inauguration of January 20, 02017, we have moved into a new time zone: the Twilight Zone.

And the Doomsday Clock just moved again in 2018.
https://blog.tutuhockey.com/2019/09/doomsday-clock.html
1

There are some Americans who sincerely thought a game show host could run America. Some voters that I know personally wanted to see things blow up.

I have friends that are literally scared for their lives now.
I think NOW they realize how they were: Bigly wrong.
Drain the Swamp? Try bulldozing.

1. Tick Tock Tick Tock Tick Tock

I don't think a narcissistic celebrity has enough knowledge to be the president of anything.

...except Denzel – he can be anything

My FIVE Rules

Rule #1

Raise your vibration

(if it's TV or any other media or technology or a cell phone, if it feels dark to you, turn it off. NOW, please.)

Rule #2

Learn CODE (or create one)

Rule #3

Opportunity? Do you have this? Do you need this?

Then shoot me an email: tracelara@protonmail.com

I have one opportunity for you in Oklahoma.

Rule #4

Get involved! Are you a teacher or parent? Host a screening of the TED talk "How a Handful of Companies Control Billions of Minds Every Day" by Tristan Harris.   https://humanetech.com/ get-involved/ HERE

Rule #5

Force yourself

FORCE YOURSELF to feel happy – as in silly goofy crazy happy! Even if you're not – PRETEND!

Give it 5 minutes each day. Do it for me and for you.

*** (My Brain on tRump)

The internet is one big toothpaste aisle and you and I are toothless.
   Bombarded with TMI? FOMO? (read Rule #1)
   Does every human being need weapons training?
   Is weather weaponized?
   Hand-Me-Downs? Somebody's gotta do serious upcycle on bad ideas.
   Baby Steps America? You are now walking backwards.
   There are 17 spy agencies doing surveillance now. How many bad guys can there be?
   Steal Trump's oxygen. Don't watch him on TV.
   Put a chimp in every press seat at the White House briefing. See what happens.

***

> "It's almost bizarre, but I also feel like poetry is a much easier way of communicating with the dead. You can recite something that resonates with you into the air and it seems like you are sending it to your loved one."
>
> *Edwidge Danticat*

LIT
HUB

the news is yelling

> The world owes you nothing. It was here first. —Mark Twain

Every day since Trump was elected feels like 9-11, over and over again. This time it is daily.

She decided to free herself, dance into the wind, create a new language. And birds fluttered around her, writing "yes" into the sky.

The news is yelling.

Watch me. Watch me.

Mass Surveillance

What is the end game — Mass Hysteria? Panic? Depression? War?

Are we part of some experiment?

It's so easy to die but so fucking hard to be alive, right?

Who feels safe? Fear spreads like fire.

Americans are as guilty as the rest of the world, in that we feel so powerless to stop mad leaders.

But we are not powerless. We are divided… on purpose.

What is ~~wrong~~ with this world? What is ~~right~~ with this world? The curse is lifting.

Hard heads.

Hard lessons.

"When a mother is forced to choose between the child and the culture, there is something abhorrently cruel and unconsidered about that culture. A culture that requires harm to one's soul in order to follow the cultures prescriptions is a very sick culture indeed. This 'culture' can be the one a woman lives in, but more damning yet, it can be the one she carries around and complies with within her own mind….."

—Women Who Run With The Wolves by Clarissa Pinkola Estes

Pink Pirates + Naming Names + Bombs

Pink Pirates
   Now that's a good name
   I think of little girls
   with paper swords made of shiny stuff
   tea cups and sparkling gowns
   and instead of killing people
   we'd grow into brave wise women
   Sign me up

Naming Names: just a few nicknames I picked up
Princess Bubble Butt
Spacy T
Lost Bird (orphan)
Three Feathers
Fancy Pants
T-Harmony
Sleeps with Knives
Tracy-ka-la-la
Winyan Ohmanisa Waste La Ke
Laura Jean Thrall on a missing piece of paper
Tracy Ann DeMeyer
Earl's daughter
Lethal Journalist
"Trace" Lara Hentz
Laramie Harlow
Woodstocker
Cold Face
Happy Girl
Herb's Wife
**
My child is your child.

Your child is my child.
All children belong to all of us.
They **all** matter.
Every bomb dropped kills a child and children.
THIS matters.
THIS ends NOW.

I confess

> To practice any art,
> no matter how well or badly,
> is a way to make
> your soul grow.
> So do it.
>
> Kurt Vonnegut

-
- I play spider solitaire a lot more than I should (but it helps me think, process, space out and time travel)

- I used to play Angry Birds on my Kindle (again it helps me think and shoot nasty pigs which is very cathartic) (I sold the Kindle a long time ago but I still miss Angry Birds.)

- I had to make up confessions when I was a kid, forced into this dark tight wood booth with a priest who often drank too much with my parents on weekends. (That same priest who wanted to marry my mom. So he could have been my dad.)

- I can't even remember how to go to confession now (lapsed Catholic that I am) and this will cost me 10 Hail Mary's I am so sure!

- I confess this is the best I have ever felt emotionally and spiritually.

- I confess uterine cancer surgery was the biggest test so far, in May 2018.

- I confess that I read books and blogs and work on other blogs when I should be fighting dust bunnies and making beds or dinner.

- Kilduff is a family name. I also have a relative named "Black Paddy" Ryan who is from Limerick, along with Kilduff relatives probably living somewhere in Eire right now. My confession is I want to meet one of them before I cross over and take the westbound on the Milky Way.

- I am a list-making fool ...Usually on post-its

lists

- make a list
- check that list
- do that list
- I'm too busy list
- oh, god, I hate this list

old photos

THE CATHOLIC HERALD CITIZEN

Planning Cathedral junior high school's first 1970 social event, a combination pizza party and dance scheduled for October, are newly elected student council members, from left, Colleen McDonough, secretary; Rob Moodie, president; Tracy DeMeyer, vice president; Charles Newman, treasurer, and Linda De

how much I changed

I have met quite a few adoptees who can't talk about being adopted. Why? They can't put feelings into words. They didn't talk about it as a kid and they never learned how to talk about it as an adult.

They might be as confused as I was when I was a child hearing that I was adopted—this was before first grade. What did "adopted" mean?

Somehow I got it—these were not my parents, someone else was. But who? And why?

I got used to hearing we "adopted" Tracy.

They'd explained I had a different mother and father. I don't think I took the news well at all. I sat with it a long time. All I could imagine was "bad." Nothing good. Something bad happened or else I wouldn't be there. Later I was very pissy and unhappy about it. I don't remember exactly how I acted but I do remember my a-mom Edie would tell me I didn't like her. I never recall saying to her "I want to go home and leave here" but I would have acted out my hurt and confusion, because I had no words for what I was feeling! She took it that I didn't like her. (Which was the groundwork for guilt which I did feel…)

Now that we have the internet and many new ways to find useful information, I read adoptees are more traumatized than a prisoner of war. That's right. It's called PTSD: post-traumatic stress disorder. A prisoner of war may escape or be released, but an adoptee may suffer their entire life.

(The following FOUR TRAUMAS is taken from my memoir *ONE SMALL SACRIFICE*)

I believe there are four distinct traumas in being an adoptee. They are: 1) in utero, when you feel what is happening to you or sense what is coming; 2) when you are delivered, abandoned, and handed to strangers; 3) later when you are told you are adopted and realize **fully** what it means; and 4) when you realize you are different, from a different culture or country, and you can't contact your people, or know them, or have the information you need to find them.

It took me years to get this. (The adrenals do go into over-drive, the fight-or-flight syndrome.)

Some adoptees are scared silent—they are not able to communicate any emotions they feel. This is the adoption fog.

Then some adoptees are afraid to meet their birthparents—afraid to know why they were given up as babies.

Then we fear we might disappoint them! (Or in my case, I had no tools when I was told by my b-mother to never contact her again. How was I supposed to handle that?)

There are more traumas, too, that happen as you age—like when I'd fill out forms at the doctor's office. I had no medical history. I had no idea if I was sitting next to someone who could be my biological brother, sister, mother or father. In my 20s it was terrifying to think I could marry my own relative! I could carry a gene or trait that I might pass down to my children—and I wouldn't know until it's too late. If my birth-parents were alcoholics (they were), then I really shouldn't drink. I could be predisposed to diabetes or heart disease or cancer or depression and not even know. My list went on and on.

In 2006, I found out my birthmother Helen Eleanor Thrall had diabetes, another shock. I never knew anything about my mother's side until the 1990s, then I met my dad Earl Hiram Bland when I was 38 in 1994.

Today I realize a powerful link exists between what I'm feeling and what happens in my body. There may be some adoptees who do not wish to face all this and go on as they are, holding on to these sad feelings and self-pity, rather than do the mental work to heal and go into reunions. Recognizing a pattern of belief is tough, partly because you gain sympathy by stealing (or sucking) energy from others when you act sick. Some call this co-dependent behavior. That is no way to live. You need to be your own person, self-energizing, and emotionally stable.

Some adoptees believe that when we meet first mother or father, all pain and agony will disappear. That sadly is just hope. That is not the way it works. A reunion is just one step on the journey and it helps, but there are many many more steps just as difficult. It's truly a test to get better.

Regardless of your ancestry, blood or skin color, adoptees can heal this. But the only one who can fix you is YOU.

about the author

I'm not really OK (just angrier)

I got a call from my good friend Bobby (I write about him in *The Whore is Home*). He just reread my memoir and asked if I'm OK.

I had to think about that. People who read my 2012 memoir ONE SMALL SACRIFICE might wonder how I survived all that: tragic childhood, abuse, the adoption crap, the bad marriage, bad everything, my search for my parents, not meeting my mother Helen, then all the research I did for TWO WORLDS, then the entire book series on Lost Children.

I can say that on most days I'm OK. I'm over with what happened because it's over. I'm not there anymore. If I reread ONE SMALL SACRIFICE again myself, I might have the same questions he did = how did I survive that?

I can only say I'm OK now because I worked on myself a very long time. I dug up the dark past so it could be exposed to light.

I didn't write every gory detail because some of it is still buried (deep)—and it needs to stay buried because I can't handle it. I don't want to remember some of it. I wrote what I could, as much as I could.

When I was in my early 20s, I had no idea back then that I would ever be OK.

And I am not OK. I'm angry. But I am getting better and healthier.

***

Trace Lara Hentz (made an honorary member of the Talligewi Sovereign Nation) is an award winning journalist. Her memoir One Small Sacrifice (2nd edition, 2012) was retired in 2018 and she plans to work on it more and un-retire it eventually. Known for her in-depth interviews for national Native newspaper NEWS FROM INDIAN COUNTRY, she won many awards, authored many academic papers, and co-edited the acclaimed book series *Lost Children of the Indian Adoption Projects.* [www.blog.americanindianadoptees.com]

In addition to her own chapbooks of poetry, *Sleeps With Knives (2nd edition in 2019) and Becoming (retired)*, Trace has also contributed to a number of publications: "What I Know" in *Spirit in the Woods*; "The Silence is So Loud" in *Invoking the Muse*; "Your God Doesn't Forget" displayed in the Memphis Brooks Museum of Art in Tennessee in 2006; "Your God Doesn't Forget," "People Waking Up," and "Heart-shaped Ass, beauty in pounds" in *Yellow Medicine Review*; "Jump" in *Rabbit and Rose*; "Earth's Funeral," "Swallow Manifesto" and "Heart-shaped Ass" in *I Was Indian Vol. 2.*; and "Swimmer" in *30 Poems in November*.

NEW: Cloud Women's Quarterly Spring 2019
Three poems were posted Cloud Women's Quarterly!

Ghost Shell placed second in national poetry contest in July of 2010. Written in May and submitted on June 23, 2010 to the Goodreads "Poetry" Contest, the poem took second place among

6 finalists on July 2. Goodreads and the "Poetry" judges Wendy Babiak, Andrew Haley, and Ruth Bavetta selected six poems as finalists and the July winner was determined by online votes. Their newsletter is distributed monthly to more than 2.5 million people. (*Ghost Shell* is published in her twin books Mental Midgets | Musqonocihte.)

Her poem "Swallow Manifesto" was published in ***Tending the Fire: Native Voices and Portraits*, by Chris Felver, in 2017.**

She has contributed writing to *Last Real Indians* and *Dissident Voice.*

Trace launched the publishing collective Blue Hand Books launched in 2011, to pay it forward, and assist other Native authors to publish their works.

She is a multi-genre author, poet, journalist and activist. Her work is heavily focused on Native Americans and Native American adoption issues. She has three unpublished theatrical plays, two fiction manuscripts underway, and an unpublished children's book series *Red Man.* In addition Trace (as poet) is thinking about***Psycho Playboys*** as a theme for a new work.

Author blog: [www.blog.tracehentz.com]

WIKI BIO: https://en.wikipedia.org/wiki/**Trace_DeMeyer**

AUTHOR

Honor Restored, Jim Thorpe's Olympic Medals (Chapter 2, pages 38-50) OLYMPICS AT THE MILLENNIUM: POWER, POLITICS AND THE GAMES 2000, Edited by Kay Shaffer and Sidonie Smith, Rutgers Press, 2000, ISBN:0-8135-2819-4
ONE SMALL SACRIFICE: A Memoir, Lost Children of the Indian Adoption Projects ISBN: 978-0-557-25599-3. 1st edition, January 2010. Book of the Month, Native America Calling, March 2010. 2nd Edition, 2012, Blue Hand Books
Co-editor: *Unraveling the Spreading Cloth of Time*: Indigenous Thoughts Concerning the Universe by MariJo Moore and Trace

A. DeMeyer (Editors) Renegade Planet Publishing, 2013

Lost Children of the Indian Adoption Projects (4 vol. book series)
Mental Midgets | Musqonocihte Twin Books: "It's a Miracle We
Survived This Far" ISBN: 9781731074010, 2019

Trace (formerly DeMeyer) lives at the foot of the Berkshire
Mountains in Greenfield Massachusetts with her fun husband/
fisherman/bowler, a retired college administrator, Herb Hentz.

my junk + blog experiments + Naked Jesus + books

Naked Jesus? Oh, hell, I write down everything

> The American Indian Adoptees blog (on Google Blogger) was created in late 2009 after my memoir *One Small Sacrifice*, and it's in the top 100 adoption blogs in 2019 (1 million+ views): http://blog.americanindianadoptees.com/
>
> In January 2011, I began to blog and write about relevant Native news and the book series Lost Children of the Indian Adoption Projects: www.laratracehentz.wordpress.com
>
> In November 2011, I founded BLUE HAND BOOKS, a collective publishing company for Native American writers, where new writers find new audiences. Books by others include Pointing with Lips, Ojibwe Hunter, Writer on the Storm, and Finding Balance. Website: www.bluehandbooks.org
>
> Starting in 2012, I taught workshops on SOCIAL MEDIA 101 (the top social media websites) and INTRODUCTION TO Google BLOGGER at Greenfield Community College in the Adult Learning Division.
>
> *Trace consults and has helped several people set up a wordpress blog, including a New York filmmaker, a Native search angel for adoptees, two new authors and a local Farmers coop to create their own blog/website using WordPress.com (the free format).*

What started you blogging?

I had to start a blog when my first book ONE SMALL SACRIFICE was published in the late fall of **2009**. If you have a book, you MUST have a blog. I have so many going I can't keep track sometimes. I had to learn Blogger and WordPress.

OK, let me list them: American Indian Adoptees on Blogger https://blog.americanindianadoptees.com/, Big BOOM Big BOOM (now dead as a doornail/hacked with a bomb), Tutu Hockey/Has it hit you yet? https://blog.tutuhockey.com/, THE BIG ISMS (formerly The Mix) https://www.thebigisms.com/, and yes a few more… There were many I made as an experiment like *Thought Bomb* and *Home Meets Dwell*.

And I wrote on the Lost Daughters blog (not too often.)

* See what I mean? There are so many!

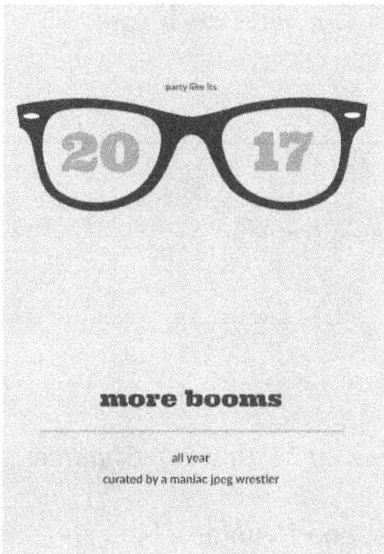

Boom was hacked and I cried.

Do you worry about how your blogs affect others?

I don't worry anymore but I did when I first started blogging.

Where do you write?

I write in a small office which is also my library.

Where do you get your ideas from?

Ideas pop into my head all the time—and I read a variety of things to get inspired. Real Life inspires me, like the true story about **Naked Jesus** who stalled traffic on I-95 and caused Herb's fishing charter boat to delay it's trip a few hours in Hyannis. Those kind of things make me think, *AH, sure, I could write about that*!

Or this scary backfire: the revelation that Bill Gates' plan to kill off mosquitoes in Brazil "backfired," and instead created a new mutant super-species far most dangerous than the native breeds. WHAT? NO? Yes!

What do you do to soothe your soul?

Writing has always helped me sort out and process my feelings. It still does.

What's one of your favourite books?

The *Outliers* by Malcolm Gladwell (but there are many many more.)

What are you searching for?

I am not searching like I used to. I'm in the moment.

What's one thing you can't live without?

My husband!

Introvert or Extrovert?

I was an extrovert until I healed my soul.

Favorite place to write?

Near running water like the ocean… it helps me breathe.

Code Name: Eltyody (Secret Sunner)

Books ::: Contributor as an adoptee:

Adoption Reunion in the Age of Social Media: *My Chapter: Finding Earl*

I contributed to this new book (Adoption Reunion). I am an adoptee who made the journey back to my first family and I share the personal details of my reunion. I am thrilled to see Laura's anthology hit bookstores and ebook readers. The topic of Adoption Reunion is very complicated, knowing millions of adoptions took place in this past century. Today, millions of adopted children are now adults with the need to know how to navigate this journey, to find relatives, ancestry, ethnicity, answers… How others successfully find and reunite with their natural families is hardly written about… The essays in this new book are REAL and as important and as varied as the subject of adoption reunion. If you plan to adopt, I only ask that you read this book and make an informed decision. If you are a birthparent, read this book. If you are a foster parent, read this book. Adoptee's voices are honored in this book. My thanks to Laura and all the contributors for making adoption reunion a priority and a reality. It was the right time for THIS book!

Lost Daughters anthology: Trace contributed a Chapter*MENDING THE HOOP*...Lost Daughters: Writing Adoption from a Place of Empowerment and Peace (anthology) The Lost Daughters anthology features a collection of writings aimed to bring readers the perspectives of adopted women and highlight their strength, resiliency, and wisdom. Amanda Woolston is the primary editor for this anthology was published through CQT Media and Publishing and LGA, Inc. in January 2014. [Kindle Edition].

Adoptionland: From Orphans to Activists [Ever wondered what it's like to be adopted? This anthology begins with personal accounts and then shifts to a bird's eye view on adoption from domestic, intercountry and transracial adoptees who are now adoptee rights activists. Along with adopted people, this collection also includes the voices of mothers and a father from the Baby Scoop Era, a modern-day mother who almost lost her child to adoption, and ends with the experience of an adoption investigator from Against Child Trafficking. These stories are usually abandoned by the very industry that professes to work for the "best interest of children," "child protection," and for families. However, according to adopted people who were scattered across nations as children, these represent typical human rights issues that have been ignored for too long. For many years, adopted people have just dealt with such matters alone, not knowing that all of us—as a community—have a great deal in common.]

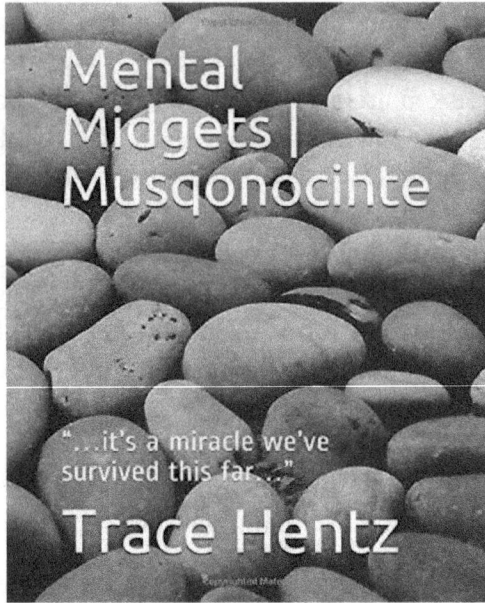

Mental Midgets | Musqonocihte Twin
Books: "It's a Miracle We Survived This
Far" ISBN: 9781731074010, 2018

Thanks

Blue Hand Books

For my family and friends and readers, I thank you. You mean
the world to me.

In memory of my sisters who changed my life:
Teresa Bland-Kiser
Victoria Cross
Ellowyn Locke
Karen Vigneault
Cindy Standing Soldier Lammers
Gay Meyers

from Becoming (an earlier work)

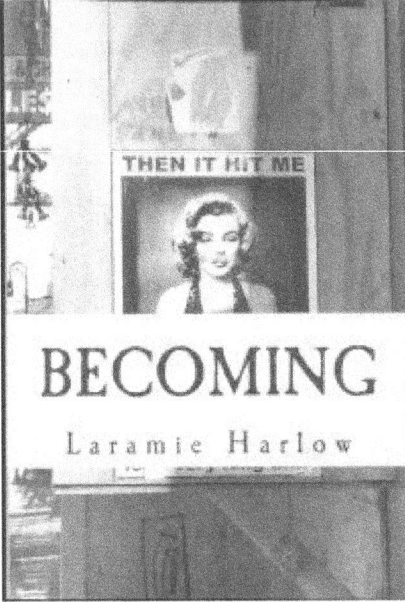

Becoming, my earlier chapbook, is now retired, out of print.

Some of the poems are included here in this new edition of SLEEPS WITH KNIVES

Where is Leo Zeck?

Leo Zeck, his student film and me

SUPERIOR, WISCONSIN 1977

Long time ago I was in a student film (at the University of Wisconsin-Superior) about a girl who walked forward while everyone was walking backwards. (I KNOW, IT WAS A CLEVER GOOD IDEA)

Folklore: Don't walk backwards.

So I did walk backwards for the short quirky film (filmed around Duluth and Superior) but that was in the late 70s. It wasn't easy, let me tell you!

Kinda glad I didn't know the folklore about this before filming.

I don't have a clue if this movie exists anywhere but Leo Zeck, if you read this, email me! [tracelara@protonmail.com]

New York New York

EARLIER IN NEW YORK CITY

When I was 23, I moved from Washington State to New York City to get into show business. My college classmate BJ's mom was an agent for actors and singers. I wrote Shirley and asked if could live with them in Queens until I got settled and employed as an actress-model-singer. She said, "Yes!"

For fast money I was employed by Elaine Newman's Model's Service and modeled shoes, sweaters and jeans. Back then earning $100 a day was like a million bucks… well to me anyway. (And I was able to buy clothes at a greatly reduced price.)

Soon I was working at the Kona Tiki as a hostess (in the Sheraton Hotel, 163 W. 52nd St) when I met singer-actor-model Daniel Drake who was also a healer-reflexologist. Dan explained about mystics like Edgar Cayce and over time he took me to some of the best bookstores in Manhattan. I read every single book by or written about Edgar Cayce over the years.

At the Kona Tiki, I worked for Cynthia Kipness who was daughter of Broadway producer "Famous" Joe Kipness who had his own restaurant Old Joe's Pier 52 across the street. My agent Shirley kept me busy working for her, delivering contracts, driving her around, auditioning and singing. Cynthia was Shirley's friend. That's how I got the very cool job and met some very high-powered people. I went on a date with comedian Dick Capri who introduced me to Rodney Dangerfield! I went with Dick to the infamous Friar's Club. I sang acapella "The Way We Were" at a famous French restaurant. I had an agent Stanley Flato who said I should be on the big screen—he tried to place me with a band from Brazil—Jose Ferrer and the Highlights who did USO tours.

All this changed me. New York City has its own power like a vortex. I was lucky to get an agent but in the process I had make-believe friends who wanted Shirley to be their agent, too. It was like a war was going on between actors. Not nice. I celebrated my 24th birthday with Dan. By late November, I was on the Greyhound back to the midwest. Let's just say, I met scary people, too.

BUT WAIT! My mind was opened. That is a good age to start questioning what you know, or think you know.

Theory, ideas, spirituality, etc. are just that: **theory.**

About the Publisher

www.bluehandcollective.com
STOP AND SMELL THE ROSES
THEN go read some REALLY great books

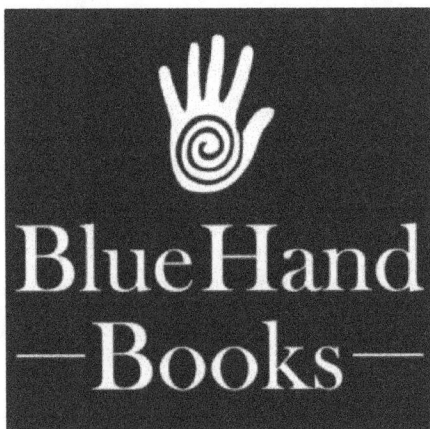
Blue Hand
—Books—

Blue Hand Books is a non-profit collective of Native American and First Nations authors based in western Massachusetts, founded in 2011.

Our Authors receive 100% of their book royalties.

www.bluehandbooks.org

Email:

bluehandcollective@outlook.com

Please help us out and tell your friends and relatives about these books. Thank YOU!

Mental Midgets | Musqonocihte | One Small Sacrifice

Laura Weldon
5.0 out of 5 stars
Lifting Truth

March 21, 2019

Combine Frank Waln's truth, Lyla June's spirit, Supaman's energy and you might get close to Lara's fiercely beautiful voice. She has been forced through the sieve of many names, but she presses on, sings for herself and for many. It is code, she says, in this book's first pages. She lets the reader decode the mystery.

When Lara lifts John Trudell's voice she lifts her own. "We're not taught about our personal relationship to power. We're not taught about our relationship to the Great Spirit. Recognizing power is what you have to do. When you recognize it, you exercise it. You can't take back what they have already taken but you can stop the taking of your power, once you recognize it." She lifts her own voice as she investigates the absence of Indian history, the erasure of Indian lives, the loss of Indian identity in many ways including adoption. Lara lifts mostly directly through her poetry in "Masks" and "I Shook" and "When a trickle… becomes a river.. then a flood" and "I Wasn't Ready For Her To Die" and most powerfully in "Ghost Shell." It's hard to leave the impact of her words behind. She writes, "a good poet would never let a good catastrophe go to waste." She shares the Hopi prophecy, "Now is the time, we are the ones we have been waiting for." In all her powerful, hip-hop-like words, her closing statements resonate. In them Lara writes, "All our suffering is mutual. All our healing is mutual. All our thriving is mutual."

? **Laura Grace Weldon is the brilliant poet author of BLACKBIRD and Ohio's poet laureate 2019**

**

Mental Midgets/Musqonocihte
By Trace Hentz
Blue Hand Books (2018)
Book Review by Dr. Stuart Bramhall

This exquisite little book is actually two books in one – both thoughtful compilations of original poems, prose snapshots, memes, photos and "creative nonfiction," all beautifully laid out on the page.

Mental Midgets contains a moving tribute to Native American musician, poet, philosopher and activities John Trudell, who died in 2015.

General themes covered in both books are colonization, the survival and resistance of indigenous people and the attitude of hopeful resistance all of us need to survive the barbarity and insanity of advanced industrial capitalism.

There are also thought-provoking quotations from fellow dissidents Noam Chomsky, Michael Moore, Lev Tolstoy, Chris Hedges, Kurt Vonnegut and Neil Young.

It's the type of book I envision re-reading repeatedly over coming months and years.

**

BOOK REVIEW:

Trace A. DeMeyer's book *One Small Sacrifice: Lost Children of the Indian Adoption Projects* is a marvelous read.

Trace narrates her story of growing up in small-town Wisconsin,

US, with her younger brother, JW and a very dysfunctional adoptive family, yet the only family she knows. What's interesting about this book is how Trace takes the reader along with her on her journey. At times I felt I was with Trace, in her house struggling with abuse, listening from the back room as her parents and parish priests drank into the wee hours. I was sitting in the bar where she and her band were performing. I was also with her when she relentlessly searched for her family of birth. I pondered with her as she tried to make sense of her home environment – disturbed, abusive adoptive father, distracted adoptive mother – and a deep desire to know her roots and connect emotionally and physically with her sorely absent parents.

One Small Sacrifice: Lost Children of the Indian Adoption Projects, provides a realistic representation of the pieces of identity that are missing year after year for those separated from their parents and tribe, as well as the laws, societal myths and pressures that require adopted children to play the role of daughter or son to those unrelated to them. There is a subtle message to readers how adopted persons, by being adopted and legally forbidden to know who they are adapt to their surroundings, while unwittingly abetting in the crime of secrecy of their own identity and past.

The reader struggles with Trace as she tries to cope with and overcome her constant questioning of all that is strange about human nature, but knowing instinctively not to blame herself for the perverse actions of others. We then share her appreciation for all the beauty in nature that is so often unnoticed. Trace shows us how to unearth the exquisiteness in birds, snakes, water and trees.

Trace is a writer, a very introspective and musical person; she has determination and a untamed spirit that keeps her moving bit by bit to find her truth, and the truth of her Indian-self and of her people who have suffered en masse through the controlling and untiring hands of the white man.

This book will help those who wonder how an adopted person is connected to an adoptive family, simply by "being there" and how complex it is to amalgamate one's adoptive identity into a found identity, and how the mind plays tricks on you when paradoxically wishing for, yet accepting the life that is and the life that never was.

Madame Compassionateless Blog

www.ingramcontent.com/pod-product-compliance
Lightning Source LLC
Chambersburg PA
CBHW031516040426
42445CB00009B/250